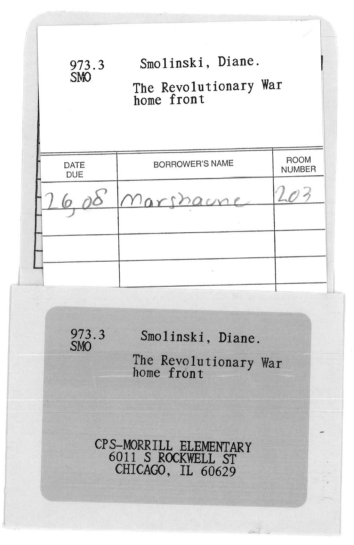

973.3
SMO   Smolinski, Diane.

The Revolutionary War
home front

DATE DUE	BORROWER'S NAME	ROOM NUMBER
26,08	Marshacne	203

The
Revolutionary War
Home Front

Diane Smolinski

Series Consultant:
Lieutenant Colonel G.A. LoFaro

Heinemann Library
Chicago, Illinois

Designed by Herman Adler Design
Printed in Hong Kong

06 05 04 03 02
10 9 8 7 6 5 4 3 2 1

Library of Congress Cataloging-in-Publication Data

Smolinski, Diane, 1950-
    The Revolutionary War Home Front / Diane Smolinski.
        p. cm. -- (Americans at War: The Revolutionary War)
Includes bibliographical references and index.
    ISBN 1-58810-277-7 (lib. bdg.)
    ISBN 1-58810-558-X (pbk. bdg.)
    1. United States--History--Revolution, 1775-1783--
Social aspects--Juvenile literature. 2. United States--
History--Revolution, 1775-1783--Causes--Juvenile
literature. 3. United States--Social conditions--To
1865--Juvenile literature. [1. United States--History--
Revolution, 1775-1783. 2. United States--Social
conditions--To 1865.] I. Title.
    E209 .S6738 2001
    973.3'1--dc21

                                    2001001616

Acknowledgments
The author and publishers are grateful to the
following for permission to reproduce copyright
material: p. 5, 6, 7 right, 13 bottom, 15 bottom, 22, 27
The Granger Collection, New York; p. 7 left, 12, 13 top,
14, 19, 20, 21, 24, 25, 29 right North Wind Picture
Archives; p. 8 Joseph Sohm/Visions of America/Corbis;
p. 9 bottom, 26, 29 left Bettmann/Corbis; p. 10, 11, 16,
Corbis; p.15 top, 17, 28 left Peter Newark's Military
Pictures; p. 18 The Newport Historical Society (P999);
p. 23 Courtesy, University of Notre Dame Libraries,
Department of Special Collections; p. 28 right Mansell/
TimePix.

Cover photograph © The Granger Collection,
New York

Every effort has been made to contact copyright
holders of any material reproduced in this book. Any
omissions will be rectified in subsequent printings if
notice is given to the publisher.

About the Author
Diane Smolinski is a teacher for the Seminole
County School District in Florida. She earned B.S.
of Education degrees from Duquesne University and
Slippery Rock University in Pennsylvania. For the past
fourteen years, Diane has taught the Revolutionary
War curriculum to fourth and fifth graders. Diane
has previously authored a series of Civil War books
for young readers. She lives with her husband, two
daughters, and their cat, Pepper.

Special thanks to Jim and Carol Fitch for their support
and interest in this project.

About the Consultant
G.A. LoFaro is a lieutenant colonel in the U.S. Army
currently stationed at Fort McPherson, Georgia. After
graduating from West Point, he was commissioned in
the infantry. He has served in a variety of positions
in the 82nd Airborne Division, the Ranger Training
Brigade, and Second Infantry Division in Korea.
He has a Masters Degree in U.S. History from the
University of Michigan and is completing his Ph.D
in U.S. History at the State University of New York
at Stony Brook. He has also served six years on the
West Point faculty where he taught military history
to cadets.

Some words are shown in bold, **like this.**
You can find out what they mean by looking in the glossary.

Contents

Colonies Are Formed

In the 1700s, various European rulers owned **territories** in North America. They often gave this land to friends or to important citizens of their home countries. These European citizens, along with others willing to make the long and dangerous journey, then crossed the Atlantic Ocean and settled this land in North America. They came in search of religious freedom, wealth, adventure, or freedom to express their opinions.

Most people who made this journey became farmers. Others were **artisans, merchants,** fishermen, or shipbuilders. Some came as **indentured servants** to escape poverty or prison. Africans were forced to cross this same ocean to be sold as slaves. These new **immigrants** formed thirteen separate **colonies** on the east coast of North America.

From Thirteen Colonies to One Nation

Originally, the colonies were ruled by several different European nations. Later, Great Britain controlled all thirteen colonies. In the early 1760s, many colonists felt British rule was unfair. This led to a war between the British and the colonists.

The boundaries of the original thirteen colonies were not the same as the states today. Of the thirteen colonies, Virginia was the first permanent European settlement in 1607. Georgia was the last to be settled in 1733.

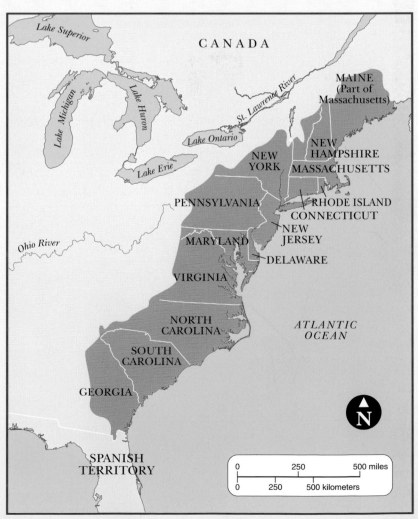

People from many different backgrounds needed to work together for this new nation to succeed.

Lives were torn apart by the fighting, and colonists were becoming more interested in a new system of government, called **democracy.** In the end, citizens had to adjust from being under the control of the British to being independent. They had to adjust from being separate colonies to being one nation. In this way, the American Revolutionary War, or the American War of **Independence,** touched the lives of all the colonists.

Town Crier News

• Many religious groups came looking for a safe place to practice their faith. Pilgrims and Puritans primarily settled in the northeastern colonies. Many Catholics from Great Britain came to Maryland. Quakers settled in Pennsylvania.

• In 1626, the Dutch bought the island of Manhattan in New York from a group of Native Americans. Many Dutch people also settled in the neighboring colonies of Delaware and New Jersey.

• Many German immigrants came to Pennsylvania and New York.

• Many other people came to North America from Europe to start the colony of Georgia.

5

British Rule of the Colonies

By 1733, the thirteen **colonies** along the Atlantic Ocean in North America belonged to a powerful British Empire. From 3,000 miles (4,828 kilometers) away, the British King and the British **Parliament** ruled these colonies. The King sent governors to the colonies to represent him. Governors were responsible for local communities obeying the king's laws.

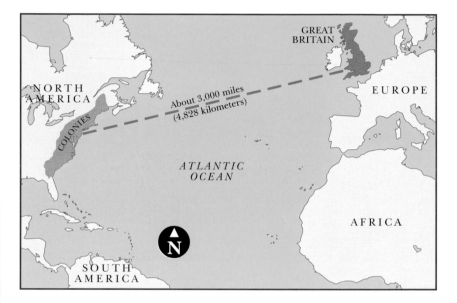

Town Crier News

• One of the reasons it was difficult for Britain to rule the colonies was that it took about two months for news to cross the Atlantic Ocean.

• British Parliament was made up of two groups of lawmakers. One was called the House of Lords and the other the House of Commons.

Members of the British House of Commons were elected to help make laws and decide upon taxes in Britain and its colonies.

Colonists did participate in making some local laws. As time passed, the British government became less interested in local **political** matters and more interested in **economic** profits they could make from the colonies. Colonists thought new tax laws made by the British king were unfair. They were growing more and more unhappy with the British ruler and Parliament.

This tax stamp was issued by the British government in 1765 to be used in the North American colonies.

Political Conflict Deepens

In 1763, Great Britain finished fighting a costly war against France in North America called the **French and Indian War.** Many Native Americans, who were called Indians at that time, helped the French fight this war. The British felt that since they protected the colonies from the French, the colonists should help them pay these war debts. **Parliament** ordered that the colonies pay several new taxes. In order for British **merchants** and the government to collect all the profits, the British also insisted that all colonial goods be shipped only to Great Britain or its **territories.**

Representatives from all the colonies met to discuss these taxation laws. The First **Continental Congress** tried to get Britain to understand their feelings. They did not like having to pay taxes without being allowed to take part in government.

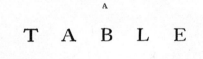

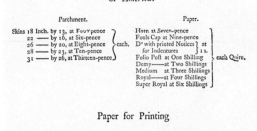

This table lists the prices of different taxes required by the British Stamp Act of 1765.

Town Crier News

- The Sugar Act of 1764 taxed molasses shipped to colonial ports. Molasses was the main sweetener used in the colonies.

- The Stamp Act of 1765 required a tax to be paid when items such as documents, licenses, and newspapers were made or sold. Each item had to be stamped as proof that the tax had been paid.

- The Townshend Acts of 1767 placed taxes on items brought into the colonies. After a few years, it was removed, except for the tax on tea.

Thoughts of Independence

Thomas Paine, a writer with an interest in politics, believed the colonies should be independent from England's rule. In a pamphlet called *Common Sense,* he explained why he felt independence and democracy were right for the North American colonies.

More and more colonists were beginning to want a government that was separate from Great Britain. However, British King George III did not plan to give the colonies what they wanted. In 1775, representatives to the Second **Continental Congress** chose a committee of five men to write a document explaining the colonists' reasons for wanting independence. On July 4, 1776, the Declaration of Independence was signed by John Hancock, president of the Continental Congress, and made available to the public.

The Declaration of Independence

By signing the Declaration, colonial **political** leaders voted to break away from British rule. The **preamble** of the Declaration explained that the document would give reasons for doing so:

Town Crier News

• Fifty-six men, representing every colony, eventually signed the Declaration of Independence.

• An early draft of the Declaration stated that slavery should not be allowed in any of the colonies. There was much disagreement on this idea, so it was taken out when the final copy was presented to the representatives.

> WHEN in the Course of human Events, it becomes necessary for one People to dissolve the Political Bands which have connected them with another, and to assume ... the separate and equal Station ... they should declare the causes which impel them to the Separation.

One reason for breaking away was that, according to the Declaration, it was the job of the government to protect everyone's basic rights of "Life, Liberty and the Pursuit of Happiness." It was also stated in the Declaration that it was wrong to be **prejudiced,** for "all Men are created equal." Great Britain, according to colonial leaders, was not protecting everyone's rights. Therefore, a government that would protect the rights of its citizens should replace it:

> Whenever any Form of Government becomes destructive ... it is the Right of the People to alter or to abolish it, and to institute new Government ... to effect their Safety and Happiness.

Benjamin Franklin from Pennsylvania, Thomas Jefferson from Virginia, John Adams from Massachusetts, Roger Sherman from Connecticut, and Robert Livingston from New York made up the group chosen to write the Declaration of Independence. The Declaration was written mostly by Jefferson and was written on parchment, a type of writing paper used at the time.

A Rebellion Begins

Not every **colonist** believed separating from Great Britain was the best plan. The Declaration of **Independence** was written in such a way as to convince them that it was. The Declaration lists 27 **abuses** by King George III of England:

> He has kept among us, in Times of Peace, Standing Armies,
>   without the consent of our Legislatures.
> For cutting off our Trade with all Parts of the World…
> For imposing Taxes on us without our Consent…
> He has plundered our Seas, ravaged our Coasts, burnt our Towns,
>   and destroyed the Lives of our People.

The colonists complained to King George, but he refused to **compromise.** The colonists felt they could no longer be loyal and must become independent of this abusive King.

> In every stage of these Oppressions we have Petitioned for Redress [the removal of the oppression] in the most humble Terms: Our repeated Petitions have been answered only by repeated Injury. A Prince, whose Character is thus marked by every act which may define a Tyrant, is unfit to be the Ruler of a free People.

King George III was crowned king of England in 1760. He wanted to be a strong ruler over the colonies.

Town Crier News

- Later in life, King George III became ill with a serious mental disease, causing him to become incapable of making decisions.

- As a result of the king's illness, his son, George IV, took over his duties.

The Beginning of a Democracy

Representatives from all the colonies wanted to have a voice in how their government operated. They wanted to make laws to live by, to be able to make enough money to take care of their families, to decide how to tax goods and services, to have trials by juries in the colonies, and to elect representatives to build a government for the people:

> We, therefore, the Representatives of the UNITED STATES OF AMERICA, in GENERAL CONGRESS, Assembled, ... solemnly Publish and Declare, That these United Colonies are, and of Right ought to be, FREE AND INDEPENDENT STATES; that they are Absolved from all Allegiance to the British Crown, and that all political connection between them and the State of Great Britain, is and ought to be totally dissolved; and that as FREE AND INDEPENDENT STATES, they have full Power to levy War, conclude Peace, contract Alliances, establish Commerce, and to do all other Acts and Things which INDEPENDENT STATES may of right do.

With this Declaration, the War for Independence began. The colonists were no longer willing to be led by a British king. Their fight for freedom would last eight years, and many parts of colonial society would help make this Declaration a reality.

Engraved by I.B.Forrest

JOHN HANCOCK,

Town Crier News

- The phrase "put your John Hancock here" means to sign your name. This saying comes from the fact that Hancock's signature stands out on the Declaration of Independence. It is near the top and is in big, bold handwriting.

- John Hancock inherited a family fortune and became a leading **merchant** in Boston, Massachusetts.

*John Hancock was the first representative at the Second **Continental Congress** to sign the Declaration of Independence.*

Small Colonial Farms

During the 1770s, most small, **colonial** farms were within 100 miles (161 kilometers) of the Atlantic Ocean. West of this was wilderness. Settlers depended on fresh water and trees to grow or build what they needed. Livestock such as chickens, pigs, cows, and sheep provided families with eggs, meat, milk, leather, and wool. Many farmers grew extra grains, vegetables, or fruits to sell to **merchants** in towns or cities.

During the Revolutionary War, farmers sold their crops to both armies. The British Army could purchase more of the available food, for British money was preferred over Continental dollars at this time. Small colonial farmers who believed in **independence** joined state **militias.** If a farmer went to war, his wife and children took care of the farm duties.

*Most small farmers did not own slaves or **indentured** servants. However, some were able to afford horses or oxen to help with plowing and hauling.*

Town Crier News

• Many Continental Army officers bought food from farmers for their troops with their own money with the promise that the Continental Army would repay them after the war.

• If a farmer sold food to the colonial armies and got caught with a large amount of Continental money, the British could charge him with **treason** for supporting the colonial rebels, even though Continental money was basically worthless. He could be put in jail, have his property taken away, or even be executed.

Farm Duties—Outside

Men and boys did most of the outside work. Men cleared fields of stones and weeds for planting, planted and harvested crops, cared for livestock, cut wood, and built fences and buildings.

Women helped the men work in the fields, especially during harvest time. They also tended vegetable gardens and milked the cows.

Children helped with the chores from a very young age. They chopped wood, gardened, and milked cows.

Farm Duties—Inside

Women did most of the work inside the home. They cleaned, cooked meals, **preserved** food, washed and sewed clothing, made quilts, and raised the children. Children often helped keep the house clean. Older children helped their mothers with such things as cooking and sewing.

All members of a small farm family helped to keep the farm running.

Plowing a new field often required moving large, heavy stones out of the way.

Town Crier News

Chopping down trees and pulling out stumps was time consuming and hard work. Native Americans taught farmers to kill the trees so that the leaves would fall off. Sunshine could then reach the crops, and farmers could plant crops close to trees. This was called "girdling."

Southern Plantations

Large farms, called plantations, were common in the southern **colonies.** Plantations grew great amounts of crops to sell. Tobacco, rice, sugar, and **indigo** were popular cash crops grown on southern plantations. Northern colonies, Europe, and the **West Indies** purchased these crops. Many workers were needed to care for these large plantations. Since family members did not work in the fields, plantation owners bought slaves to do this work.

Many plantation owners stayed loyal to the king because England was purchasing their crops. Most early battles of the Revolutionary War were fought in the northern colonies. As the war continued, the fighting moved south and plantations were damaged.

The economy of the agricultural South depended on slave labor. Without modern equipment, harvesting crops required the help of many people.

Town Crier News

- Thomas Jefferson was born on a Virginia tobacco plantation called Shadwell.

- George Washington inherited a plantation in Virginia called Mount Vernon.

Plantation Duties—Outside

Plantation owners managed the outside work. Owners decided what crops to grow, where crops would be planted, and how crops were to be sold. They also bought and sold slaves to do this outside work. Owners hired other white men to manage the slaves and carry out their planting plan.

Plantation Duties—Inside

Wives of plantation owners managed the household activities. They planned meals, arranged social activities, supervised the children, and directed the slaves who did indoor work.

Men managed the money and bookkeeping matters. Many also participated in local **political** activities, such as attending town meetings and voting.

Children often helped with chores such as cooking or cleaning, but they did little work overall. Rather than attend public schools, children who lived on plantations were taught at home by private **tutors.**

Plantation owners walked out among their slaves from time to time to observe the workers.

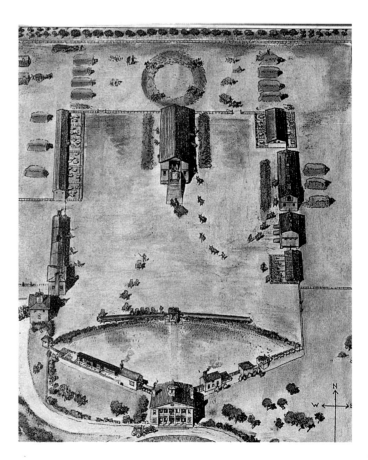

Plantations were small, self-contained cities. They had stables for horses, laundries, schools for the planters' children, and mills for grinding grain. The owner's mansion stood at the entrance of this eighteenth century Maryland plantation.

Slavery in the Colonies

As early as the 1600s, African families were forced to travel 3,000 miles (4,828 kilometers) across the Atlantic Ocean to British **colonies** in North America. Many did not survive this ocean voyage. Those who did were sold to the highest bidder as slaves. Northern **merchants** made large profits from buying and selling slaves.

Slavery was legal in the colonies. By law, anyone born to a slave automatically became a slave. Even though slaves were valuable, they were treated poorly. None had any legal rights. They received no formal education, and few had any hope of ever being anything but a slave.

Town Crier News

In 1807, an act in the U.S. Constitution made it illegal to bring slaves into the United States from Africa.

During the Revolutionary War years, slaves lived in all the colonies. Most of them worked the fields on southern plantations. Slaves also worked as servants in cities.

The slave ship Gloria, *illustrated here, was just one of many ships transporting Africans to the American colonies to be sold as slaves. Conditions on the ships were so terrible that many of the Africans did not survive the voyage.*

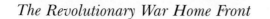

Former slaves often served in the army as grooms. They took care of the horses of military leaders. The Marquis de Lafayette and his groom are pictured here at the Battle of Yorktown, Virginia, in 1781.

Slaves Fight for the Colonies

At the beginning of the war, slaves freed by their owners could volunteer to fight. Southern representatives to the **Continental Congress** were against allowing slaves to join the Continental Army. George Washington, commander in chief of the army, was ordered to stop enlisting slaves. As the war went on, the Continental Army found itself in greater need of soldiers. Congress approved offering freedom to slaves if they served in the military. Even though military life was very difficult at this time, some slaves thought it was better to be a soldier than a slave.

Some slave owners who joined the army took their slaves with them. Others sent their slaves in place of their sons. In the South, many slave owners did not want their slaves to go to war. They were too valuable to risk losing, especially when the war was not likely to damage their property.

Town Crier News

More than 5,000 Africans, including both slaves and free men, joined the Continental Army.

Slaves Fight for the British

More slaves fought for Great Britain than for the **colonies.** The British offered freedom to slaves who joined their army or navy. Many slaves escaped from plantations to gain freedom.

In 1783, the treaty was signed that formally gave the colonies their **independence** from Britain. Many colonists demanded that Britain return all American property. They wanted the return of runaway slaves, whom they considred to be property. The acting commander of the British Army refused to do this. Slaves who had fought for the British during the war boarded British ships and traveled to British-held **territories** to begin their new lives.

Town Crier News

- One way that slaves helped the British Army was by serving as guides in unfamiliar countryside.

- Others served as cooks or took care of the horses.

Little is known about the man in this portrait. He is wearing the uniform of a full captain in the British Navy. Since it is unlikely that a former slave would have been made a captain in the British Navy at the time of the Revolutionary War, it is likely that the uniform he is wearing in this portrait was taken during a raid on a British ship.

Native Americans

As the colonies became more populated, Native Americans moved inland to less-settled land. This land was considered wilderness, even though it was barely 100 miles (161 kilometers) from the ocean.

During the Revolutionary War, both the colonists and the British wanted the support of the Native Americans. Most tribes did not choose sides in this conflict, but the tribes that did choose usually fought for the British. Native Americans expected the British to win the war. Colonial leaders also worked hard to establish peaceful relationships with the Native Americans. The colonies did not want to be fighting the Native Americans and the British at the same time.

Town Crier News

- About 13,000 Native Americans fought for the British during the Revolutionary War.

- Many Native Americans fought for the British because the British did not allow colonists to settle west of the Appalachian Mountains. The Native Americans were in favor of this because they did not want to lose any more of their land.

Tecumseh, from the Shawnee nation, was a teenager during the Revolutionary War. He was hostile toward settlers because they were taking land away from the Shawnee people. He participated in British and Indian attacks on colonists.

After the war, the British presented this medal to the chiefs of Indian tribes that had been Britain's allies.

19

Colonial Cities

In 1760, the most **populated** cities in North America were located in the northeast. About 23,000 people lived in Philadelphia, Pennsylvania. About 18,000 lived in New York City, New York. Approximately 16,000 lived in Boston, Massachusetts. Charleston, South Carolina, was the most populated city in the southern **colonies,** with about 8,000 people. All were centers of **political, cultural,** and **economic** activity.

During the Revolutionary War, the British fought the American colonies for control of these seaport cities. Cities were an important source of **revenue** for both sides.

Valuable goods came and went from busy seaports. This meant that ports, like Charleston, South Carolina, were very important to the colonies and to Great Britain.

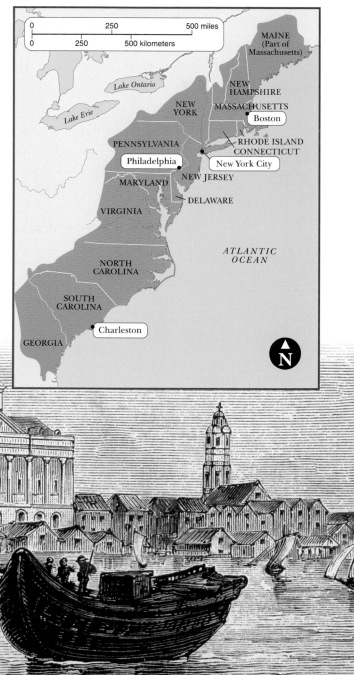

Philadelphia's large population and central location within the colonies made it an important meeting place during the time of the Revolutionary War.

Philadelphia in 1775

Philadelphia, Pennsylvania, was a typical large city of the late 1700s. It had **cobblestone** streets and brick sidewalks. Gas streetlamps brightened the walkways at night. Homes were made of brick, stone, or wood. None had running water or indoor bathrooms. Some citizens kept cows, chickens, or pigs in their yards. Public schools, a museum, a public library, and a medical school offered educational opportunities. Citizens could also attend the theater. A hospital was available for medical emergencies, and there was a prison for housing criminals.

Town Crier News

- In 1787, the U.S. Constitution was signed in Philadelphia's Independence Hall.

- From 1790 to 1800, Philadelphia was the capital city of the United States.

- By 1800, New York City was the most populated city in the United States.

A State House, later named **Independence** Hall, was a center for colonial government activity. The **Continental Congress** met there and approved the Declaration of Independence.

Philadelphia Grows and Develops

By the start of the Revolutionary War, more than 30,000 people lived in Philadelphia. It was a busy port city. Farmers delivered their crops to **merchants** who then shipped these crops to other **colonies,** Europe, or the **Caribbean.** As the city grew larger, workers were needed to build buildings. Craftsmen were in demand to make furniture and decorative items, especially for the wealthier citizens. A variety of other businesses, such as fishing, shipbuilding, and whaling, were also doing well.

During the war, British naval **blockades** disrupted activities. Trade continued, but costs were much higher.

From 1777 to 1778, the British occupied the city of Philadelphia. The colonists fought hard to keep it from British control at the Battles of Brandywine, Germantown, and Trenton.

Merchant ships frequently came and went from the port at Philadelphia.

New Jersey colonial money included this 1776 six-pound note. A "pound" is a money unit used in many countries, including Great Britain.

Money Problems

One problem for the colonists during the Revolutionary War was that the British did not allow them to make coins. Ships bringing goods from Europe and South America brought coins to the colonies. The Spanish-milled dollar soon became the most common coin in use, and the supply of available coins was not enough to fill the demand. This led the **Continental Congress** to allow the national government and each individual colony to print paper money. Each colony chose a different design and decided which **denominations** to use.

Problems arose when the Continental government and the individual colonies did not have the silver or gold to back all this paper money. Paper money soon became nearly worthless. By 1781, it could cost 350 colonial paper dollars to purchase an item that could be bought for one gold dollar coin. Finally, in 1789, the U.S. Constitution prevented states from printing their own money. From then on, only the United States government could print paper money.

Town Crier News

- Before 1777, colonial money had "United Colonies" printed on it. After 1777, it had "United States" printed on it.

- Money from the New Jersey colony had the Royal Arms of Great Britain printed on it.

- Many colonial bills for individual states were printed only on one side.

Life in the City

Many different **economic** classes of people lived in cities during the Revolutionary War. Wealthy citizens were often **merchants** who owned large businesses. These men were usually educated and often participated in politics. Middle income citizens were usually craftsmen who owned small businesses or were laborers for larger businesses. Slaves or **indentured servants** worked for wealthier citizens. Each of these different kinds of people lived in the larger cities.

Homes

Wealthy merchants generally owned roomy brick or stone houses. They bought many furnishings to decorate their homes. Most craftsmen and laborers lived in comfortable wooden homes. Many of these middle-income citizens kept cows, chickens, or pigs in sheds in their yards. They made most of the items they needed for their homes. Slaves or indentured servants did not own property. They helped care for the property of their owners.

Town Crier News

Home design was influenced by the style of the country from which the builders or owners came.

Many mansions were built in colonial cities. This Boston mansion belonged to John Hancock, one of the signers of the Declaration of Independence.

Town Crier News

There were no zippers to fasten clothing at this time. They had only buttons and drawstrings.

Clothing

Wealthy adults showed off their success by dressing stylishly. Style was important when in business meetings, entertaining, or participating in politics. Men wore breeches, or pants, that buttoned below the knee. They tucked long, woolen stockings under the breeches and wore long suit coats or waistcoats over loose-fitting shirts. Men grew their hair longer and pulled it back into a ponytail. Women wore long dresses, often covering them with aprons to protect their clothing. Dresses for special occasions were often made of silk and had layers of **petticoats** underneath. Slaves and indentured servants—who dressed in poorer quality material—were often required to mend the fine clothes of their owners.

Middle income adults dressed similarly to the wealthy. However, the cloth they used would have been less expensive. Children's clothing was similar in style to their parents' clothing.

Education

Wealthy people often sent their sons to private schools or hired **tutors.** Some girls attended schools, but most were taught at home. Girls usually learned only the skills they needed to be good wives and mothers. Girls from middle-income families most often were taught these skills by their mothers.

Less wealthy citizens went to public schools in the cities. In some cities, students were required to bring firewood to help heat the school. Slaves and indentured servants did not attend school.

Wealthy colonial ladies and gentlemen gather in a parlor for tea.

Women During the Revolutionary War

Society expected colonial women during the 1770s to care for their children and manage their households. Colonial laws were very similar to British laws. At this time, colonial women were not allowed to vote.

Some colonial women simply continued with everyday life as it was before the Revolutionary War began, but many chose to take an active part in the war. Some women hoped that the freedoms the colonies were fighting for would also apply to them. Abigail Adams was one such woman. She encouraged her husband, John, who was serving in the **Continental Congress,** to consider the needs of women as well as men when making new laws.

Abigail Adams believed that women should not have to follow laws they played no part in making. This same idea contributed to the colonists' fight for **independence** *from British rule.*

Town Crier News

- Some of Abigail's friends thought she should not marry John Adams because he was a lawyer and she was the daughter of a minister.

- Abigail Smith Adams became the **First Lady** in 1797 when her husband, John, was elected the second president of the United States.

Supporting the British Army

During the Revolutionary War, some women chose to help the British Army. Women called camp followers traveled with British troops doing laundry, mending clothes, cooking, and nursing the wounded. Some women living in the colonies even acted as spies for the British. After the war, many of these women went to live in British **territories.**

Supporting the Colonial Army

Some women, called camp followers, joined the colonial troops on the fighting fields to cook and do laundry for them. Others, such as Deborah Sampson and Rachel and Grace Martin, disguised themselves as men and joined the army. Several women, such as Lydia Darragh, were spies. When their husbands, sons, and fathers went to war, many women ran the family farms and businesses themselves.

Women often followed closely behind the armies to help out in any way they could. Female camp followers are pictured here at the Battle of Lexington on April 19, 1775.

Loyalists and Patriots

During the Revolutionary War, **colonists** who supported the British government were called Loyalists. They did not want the government to change. Those who supported the colonial cause were called Patriots. They wanted the government to gain **independence** from Great Britain.

Lieutenant Colonel Banastre Tarleton was a member of the British Legion, part of the American Loyalist cavalry.

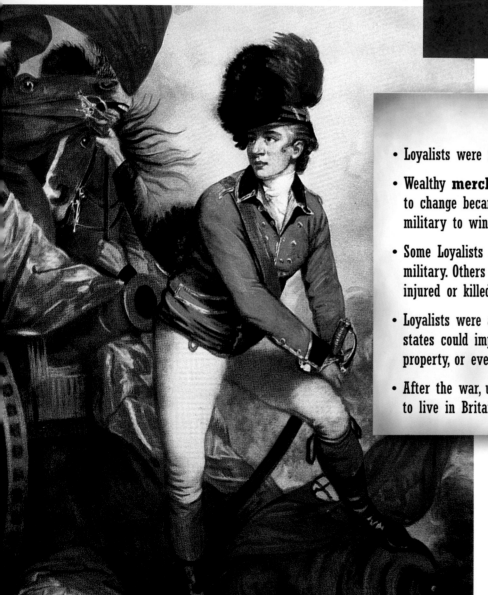

Loyalists

- Loyalists were from all different parts of colonial society.

- Wealthy **merchants** who did not want their businesses to change became Loyalists. Slaves who joined the British military to win their freedom were Loyalists.

- Some Loyalists acted as spies and served in the British military. Others lived quietly, not wanting to risk getting injured or killed in battle.

- Loyalists were at times threatened by Patriots. Individual states could impose heavy taxes on them, take away their property, or even put them in prison.

- After the war, up to 100,000 Loyalists left the colonies to live in Britain, Canada, or British **territories.**

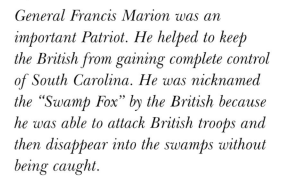

General Francis Marion was an important Patriot. He helped to keep the British from gaining complete control of South Carolina. He was nicknamed the "Swamp Fox" by the British because he was able to attack British troops and then disappear into the swamps without being caught.

Patriots

- Patriots were also from all parts of colonial society.

- Merchants who were unhappy with British laws and taxes or slaves who were promised freedom for joining colonial forces were Patriots.

- Patriots served in the military, acted as spies, or continued to quietly keep their farms and businesses running.

- Patriots were not usually threatened by the Loyalists.

- After the war, Patriots stayed in the colonies and continued farming or running their businesses.

By 1783, the Patriots had realized their dream of total independence. The Loyalists who had chosen to stay in North America would now work together with the Patriots to shape the United States of America.

Glossary

abuse   unfair action

artisan   person with a talent for doing a special job, such as woodworking or making jewelry

blockade   troops or warships that block enemy troops or supplies from entering or leaving an area

Caribbean   area of the Atlantic Ocean bordered on the north and the east by the West Indies, on the west by Central America, and on the south by South America

cobblestone   type of street made up of rounded stones

colony   territory settled by people from other countries who still had loyalty to those other countries. The word *colonist* is used to describe a person who lives in a colony. The word *colonial* is used to describe things related to a colony.

compromise   to settle a difference of opinion by having each side give in on certain parts of the issues

Continental Congress   group of representatives from the colonies who carried out the duties of the government

cultural   those ideas, customs, and manners that are in line with a shared set of values

democracy   form of government that gives the people and their elected representatives the power to make and enforce laws

denomination   specific value of a piece of money

economic   relating to how money is earned and spent or to how goods and services are produced and sold

First Lady   wife of a United States president

French and Indian War   called the Seven Years' War in Europe. From 1754 to 1763, Britain fought against France in the North American colonies. Some Native Americans—called Indians at the time—helped the French.

immigrant   person who moves permanently to one country from another

indentured servant   person who agreed to work for another for a set period of time in order to repay a debt

independence   freedom

indigo   plant that was used to make a blue dye to color cloth

merchant   person who buys and sells goods

militia   group of ordinary men who fought to protect the colonies before the Revolutionary War and then fought alongside the Continental Army during the war

Parliament   lawmakers of the British government

petticoat   underskirt worn by women in colonial times

political   having to do with the government

populated   crowded with people

preamble   opening words of a formal document

prejudice   judging another unfairly

preserve   keep from spoiling

revenue   amount of money the government collected from taxes and other sources

territory   area ruled by the government of another country

treason   attempt to overthrow the government or to harm a member of royalty

tutor   person hired to teach students on an individual basis or in a small group, often in their own homes

West Indies   group of islands between North and South America

Historical Fiction to Read

Banim, Lisa. *A Spy in the King's Colony.* New York: Silver Moon Press, 1998.
Eleven-year-old Emily Parker is living in Boston in 1775. She is a Patriot, and she
suspects her neighbor Robert of being a Loyalist spy.

Denenberg, Barry. *The Journal of William Thomas Emerson: A Revolutionary War Patriot,
Boston, Massachusetts, 1774.* New York: Scholastic, 1998.
A twelve-year-old orphan boy keeps a diary of his experiences before and during the
Revolutionary War.

Schurfranz, Vivian. *A Message for General Washington.* New York: Silver Moon Press, 1998.
A twelve-year-old girl travels from her home in Yorktown, Virginia, to bring an
important message to General George Washington.

Historical Places to Visit

Adams National Historical Park
135 Adams Street
Quincy, Massachusetts 02169-1749
Visitor Information: (617) 770-1175
Visit the place where U.S. President John Adams was born. See the family tomb in which
both John Adams and his wife, Abigail Adams, are buried.

Boston National Historical Park
Charlestown Navy Yard
Boston, Massachusetts 02129-4543
Visitor Information: (617) 242-5642
Take the Freedom Trail walking tour of the park to see sixteen Revolutionary War sites
and structures. Visit downtown Boston to see the Old State House and the Paul Revere
House. Then visit Charlestown to see the Bunker Hill Monument.

Independence National Historical Park
313 Walnut Street
Philadelphia, Pennsylvania 19106
Visitor Information: (215) 597-8974
Visit the place where the Declaration of Independence and the U.S. Constitution were
written. Tour downtown Philadelphia to see the Liberty Bell, Independence Hall, and
other historical landmarks of the Revolutionary War.

Index